The Corgi Series

IDRIS DAVIES
A Carol for the Coalfield
and other poems

The Corgi Series   *Writing from Wales*

Idris Davies

A Carol for the Coalfield
and other poems

Series editor
Meic Stephens
Professor of Welsh Writing in English
University of Glamorgan

Carreg Gwalch Cyf.

The Collected Poems of Idris Davies
is published by Gwasg Gomer.

ISBN: 0-86381-702-5

Cover design: Sian Parri
Logo design: Dylan Williams

First published in 2002 by
Carreg Gwalch Cyf., 12 Iard yr Orsaf, Llanrwst,
Wales LL26 0EH
☎ 01492 642031   📠 01492 641502
📧 books@carreg-gwalch.co.uk
website: www.carreg-gwalch.co.uk

Supported by an 'Arts for All' Lottery grant
from the Arts Council of Wales

We wish to thank Gwasg Gomer for their co-operation
in producing this volume and for their kind permission
to include material originally published by them.
Our thanks also to Gwyn and Ceinfryn Morris,
the copyright holders.

Contents

Idris Davies

Idris Davies was born in Rhymney, Monmouthshire, on 6 January 1905. The family was Welsh-speaking, as were some two thirds of the town's population in those days; the poet spoke the language fluently and wrote a little in it. He left school at the age of fourteen to become a miner at the McLaren Pit, Abertysswg, where his father was chief winderman. Having been introduced to the work of Shelley by a fellow-miner, he quickly saw that poetry could relate to politics, especially Socialism. Early in 1926 he lost a finger while working underground at the Maerdy Pit, Pontlottyn, and had barely restarted work when the General Strike began and the pit was closed.

Having taken a correspondence course, he went on to study at Loughborough College and the University of Nottingham, where he qualified as a teacher. He taught at schools in England and then in Wales, notably at Llandysul in Cardiganshire and Treherbert in the Rhondda. After many unsuccessful attempts, he obtained a teaching post at Cwmsyfiog Junior School in the Rhymney Valley in 1947 but, four years later, was found to be suffering from cancer. He died on 6 April 1953. There is a memorial plaque on the wall of 7 Victoria Road, Rhymney, his mother's house, where he died, and another in the town's public library.

His first book, *Gwalia Deserta*, published in 1938, took as its theme the desert of industrial south Wales, in particular the economic crisis of the inter-war years and the social deprivation it brought in its wake; its thirty-six sections include 'The Bells of Rhymney', a poem later set to music and made famous by the singing of Pete Seeger. His second book, *The Angry Summer* (1943), 'a poem of 1926', consisting of fifty short, untitled sections, is a loosely chronological record, with interludes, of the General Strike (4-12 May 1926) and the seven-month lock-out of the miners which followed. Its main focus is on the plight of the mining communities of south Wales, especially their womenfolk, but also on Dai, the archetypal miner who becomes the poet's *alter ego*. Both books can be considered as long, unified dramatic poems denouncing capitalism and expressing the poet's deep sympathy with his own people. His third book, *Tonypandy and other poems* (1945), finished while he was teaching at Treherbert, includes the long autobiographical poem, 'I was born in Rhymney'.

A volume of Idris Davies's *Selected Poems* appeared a few weeks before the poet's death; they were chosen by T. S. Eliot, who said of his work: 'They are the best poetic document I know about a particular epoch in a particular place, and I think they really have a claim to permanence.'

Gwalia Deserta (extracts)

II

My fathers in the mining valleys
Were slaves who bled for beer,
Who had no Saviour to acclaim
And whose god was Fear.

And they sold the fern and flower
And the groves of pine
For a hovel and a tankard,
And the dregs are mine.

So in these rain-swept graveyards
Where my fathers sleep,
Shall I sulk, and curse them
Who made their lives so cheap?

Or shall I pause, and pity
Those luckless lads of old,
Those sullen slaves whipped onward
To load my lords with gold?

IV

O timbers from Norway and muscles from Wales,
Be ready for another shift and believe in
                        co-operation,
Though pit-wheels are frowning at old misfortunes
And girders remember disasters of old;
O what is man that coal should be so careless of
                               him,
And what is coal that so much blood should be
                           upon it?

VII

There are countless tons of rock above his head,
And gases wait in secret corners for a spark;
And his lamp shows dimly in the dust.
His leather belt is warm and moist with sweat,
And he crouches against the hanging coal,
And the pick swings to and fro,
And many beads of salty sweat play about his lips
And trickle down the blackened skin
To the hairy tangle on the chest.
The rats squeak and scamper among the unused
                           props,
And the fungus waxes strong.

And Dai pauses and wipes his sticky brow,
And suddenly wonders if his baby
Shall grow up to crawl in the local Hell,
And if to-morrow's ticket will buy enough food for
six days,
And for the Sabbath created for pulpits and bowler
hats,
When the under-manager cleans a dirty tongue
And walks with the curate's maiden aunt to
church . . .
Again the pick resumes the swing of toil,
And Dai forgets the world where merchants walk
in morning streets,
And where the great sun smiles on pithead and
pub and church-steeple.

VIII

Do you remember 1926? That summer of soups and
speeches,
The sunlight on the idle wheels and the deserted
crossings,
And the laughter and the cursing in the moonlit
streets?
Do you remember 1926? The slogans and the
penny concerts,
The jazz-bands and the moorland picnics,
And the slanderous tongues of famous cities?

Do you remember 1926? The great dream and the
                                    swift disaster,
The fanatic and the traitor, and more than all,
The bravery of the simple, faithful folk?
'Ay, ay, we remember 1926,' said Dai and Shinkin,
As they stood on the kerb in Charing Cross Road,
'And we shall remember 1926 until our blood is
                                    dry.'

XII

There's a concert in the village to buy us boots and
                                    bread,
There's a service in the chapel to make us meek and
                                    mild,
And in the valley town the draper's shop is shut.
The brown dogs snap at the stranger in silk,
And the winter ponies nose the buckets in the
                                    street.
The 'Miners' Arms' is quiet, the barman half afraid,
And the heroes of newspaper columns on
                        explosion day
Are nearly tired of being proud.
But the widow on the hillside remembers a bitterer
                                    day,
The rap at the door and the corpse and the crowd,
And the parson's powerless words.

And her daughters are in London serving dinner to
my lord,
And her single son, so quiet, broods on his luck in
the queue.

XV

Oh what can you give me?
Say the sad bells of Rhymney.

Is there hope for the future?
Cry the brown bells of Merthyr.

Who made the mineowner?
Say the black bells of Rhondda.

And who robbed the miner?
Cry the grim bells of Blaina.

They will plunder willy-nilly,
Say the bells of Caerphilly.

They have fangs, they have teeth!
Shout the loud bells of Neath.

To the south, things are sullen,
Say the pink bells of Brecon.

Even God is uneasy,
Say the moist bells of Swansea.

Put the vandals in court!
Cry the bells of Newport.

All would be well if-if-if –
Say the green bells of Cardiff.

Why so worried, sisters, why?
Sing the silver bells of Wye.

XVI

We went to Cardiff when the skies were blue
And spent our shillings freely
In Queen Street and the bright arcades,
And in the cockle market.
And dainty little typists and daintier little
                                    gentlemen
Smiled most scornfully upon our cruder accents.
But we were happy unambitious men
Ready to laugh and drink and forget,
And to accept the rough and ready morrows
Of the mining valleys.
We tasted strawberries and cream,
And perhaps we thought our transient luck would
                                                    last,

And perhaps we dreamed a little in Cathays,
And we crowded into cinemas and cafés,
Or danced at evening, or sought a burning wench
And told her many tales.

And in the night, we laughed our way back home
                                                 again
In trains that whistled merrily.
And some would open carriage windows
And gaze upon the stars above the Severn plain,
And some would jest about a woman,
And some would slip into a perfect sleep.

Back in our homes, by flickering fires,
We bade the day farewell in careless language,
And sought the simple beds of happy men.

XVIII

Play dominoes till dusk, play dominoes and sigh,
For who will give you work again?
Your fists are growing tender with the years,
And all the April hopes you had
Are lifeless leaves in autumn gutters.
So call your cronies to that table by the stove
In the little Welfare Institute,
And play and talk until the valley lights are lit.
Gaze out through dusty window panes

On delicate parsons passing by,
And the children of Gwalia seeking soup.
Or call to your side some veteran, grey and scarred,
And listen to the anecdotes of Chartism
That the veteran's father told,
And listen, listen to the frantic footsteps of the past
                              When the red-coats rode to Gwalia to beat the
                                             toilers down.
But if the sun is on the valley sides,
Go lie among the hillside fern, forgetting all the
                                             gangs,
And gaze upon those distant paths of boyhood,
And praise again the glory of the mountain grass,
And love again those mountain meres and those
                              shepherds' walls.
Do you remember, as you lie among the fern,
The Sunday School, the coal-face, and the girl who
                                     teased you first?
The football that you played among the coal-tips in
                                     the evening,
The lads you laughed with on your way from
                                     work?
The times you sang with Dai in the local
                       eisteddfod,
With Dai and Glyn and Emrys, singing the songs of
                                             Zion,
Of Gilead and of Galilee?

XX

O where are our fathers, O brothers of mine?
By the graves of *their* fathers, or awaiting a sign.
The Welsh skies are sullen, and the stars are all dim,
And the dragon of Glyndwr is bruised in the limb.
The brown earth is waiting for brothers of mine
And our mothers are hanging the shrouds on
                        the line.
The deacons are groaning and the sheep-dogs
                        are thin
And Dai is in London drinking tea from a tin.

XXII

I stood in the ruins of Dowlais
And sighed for the lovers destroyed
And the landscape of Gwalia stained for all time
By the bloody hands of progress.
I saw the ghosts of the slaves of The Successful
                        Century
Marching on the ridges of the sunset
And wandering among derelict furnaces,
And they had not forgotten their humiliation,
For their mouths were full of curses.
And I cried aloud, O what shall I do for my fathers
And the land of my fathers?
But they cursed and cursed and would not answer
For they could not forget their humiliation.

XXIV

Because I was sceptical in our Sunday School
And tried to picture Jesus crawling in the
                              local mine,
The dozen deacons bred on the milk of Spurgeon
Told me I was dangerous and in danger,
That I would be roasted and pronged and tossed
                              like a pancake;
And then they would frown and go apart to pray.
On Sabbath evenings when I yawned in
                  grandmother's pew,
When the parson roused himself with his raised
                                    arms,
And the elders cried out 'Amen, Amen',
And Jenkins the Joiner nudged his wife with a
                              caramel,
And tired mothers were musing on carpets and
                        insurance agents,
And young fathers coaxed tiny boys to sleep,
I remember I used to stare through the chapel
                              windows
Watching the sun like a perfect tomato touching
                              the hill,
And a swarthy young man wandering on a
                        purple ridge,
And his body was bent and his smile was
                  compassionate.

And sometimes in mid-week I would see him
                                    again,
And we would smile and understand.

XXVI

The village of Fochriw grunts among the higher
                                    hills;
The dwellings of miners and pigeons and pigs
Cluster around the little grey war memorial.
The sun brings glitter to the long street roofs
And the crawling promontories of slag,
The sun makes the pitwheels to shine,
And praise be to the sun, the great unselfish sun,
The sun that shone on Plato's shoulders,
That dazzles with light the Taj Mahal.
The same sun shone on the first mineowner,
On the vigorous builder of this brown village,
And praise be to the impartial sun.
He had no hand in the bruising of valleys,
He had no line in the vigorous builder's plans.
He had no voice in the fixing of wages,
He was the blameless one.
And he smiles on the village this morning,
He smiles on the far-off grave of the vigorous
                                    builder,
On the ivied mansion of the first mineowner,
On the pigeon lofts and the Labour Exchange,
And he smiles as only the innocent can.

XXX

Ride you into Merthyr Tydfil
Where the fountains have run dry,
And gaze upon the sands of fortune
But pray not to the sky.

If you will to Merthyr Tydfil,
Ride unarmed of dreams;
No manna falls on Merthyr Tydfil,
And there flow no streams.

Pints of pity give no healing,
Eyes go blind that will not see,
Ride you into Merthyr Tydfil
With salt of charity.

XXXI

Consider famous men, Dai bach, consider famous
                                        men,
All their slogans, all their deeds,
And follow the funerals to the grave.
Consider the charlatans, the shepherds of the
                                        sheep!
Consider the grease upon the tongue, the hunger
                                        of the purse!
Consider the fury of the easy words,

The vulgarity behind the brass,
The dirty hands that shook the air, that stained
the sky!

Yet some there were who lived for you,
Who lay to die remembering you.

Mabon was your champion once upon a time
And his portrait's on the milk-jug yet.
The world has bred no champions for a long time
now,
Except the boxing, tennis, golf and Fascist kind,
And the kind that democracy breeds and feeds for
Harringay.
And perhaps the world has grown too bitter or
too wise
To breed a prophet or a poet ever again.

XXXIV

When we walked to Merthyr Tydfil, in the
moonlight long ago,
When the mountain tracks were frozen and the
crests were capped with snow,
We had tales and songs between us, and souls too
young to fret,
And we had hopes and visions which the heart
remembers yet.

The winds from the farthest mountains blew about
                                    us as we strode,
But we were warm and merry on the crooked
                                    freezing road,
And there were lamp-lit homesteads to south and
                                    east and west
And we watched the round moon smiling on those
                                    little lights of rest.

The moon is still as radiant and the homely hills
                                    remain,
But the magic of those evenings we shall not meet
                                    again,
For we were boyish dreamers in a world we did not
                                    know
When we walked to Merthyr Tydfil in the
                                    moonlight long ago.

XXXVI

In the places of my boyhood
    The pit-wheels turn no more,
Nor any furnace lightens
    The midnight as of yore.

The slopes of slag and cinder
    Are sulking in the rain,
And in derelict valleys
    The hope of youth is slain.

And yet I love to wander
    The early ways I went,
And watch from doors and bridges
    The hills and skies of Gwent.

Though blighted be the valleys
    Where man meets man with pain,
The things my boyhood cherished
    Stand firm, and shall remain.

The Angry Summer (extracts)

A poem of 1926

1

Now it is May among the mountains,
Days for speeches in the valley towns,
Days of dream and days of struggle,
Days of bitter denunciation.

Now it is May in all the valleys,
Days of the cuckoo and the hawthorn,
Days for splashing in the mountain ponds,
Days for love in crowded parks.

Now it is May in little gardens,
In square allotments across the railway,
Days for song and dance and roaming,
Days for action and achievement.

Now it is May in the minds of men,
Days for vision and for marching,
Days for banners and for music,
And beauty born of sacrifice.

2

From Abertillery and Aberdare
And Rhondda Fach and Rhondda Fawr
And Ogmore Vale and Nine Mile Point
And Bargoed and Brynmawr,
The delegates some in morning trains
To meet in Cardiff City,
And some have tongues and some have brains
And some pretend they're witty,
And some have come with hearts aflame
To plead and plan and fight
For those who toil without a name
And pass into the night.

4

Tonight the moon is bright and round
Above the little burial ground
Where father of Dai and father of John
After the sweat and blood sleep on.

They do not hear your voice tonight,
O singer on the slaggy height,
They do not know the song you sing
Of battle on this night of spring.

But in their blood in Maytimes past
The armies of the future massed,
And in their dreams your dreams were born,
Out of their night shall break your morn.

Shine softly, moon, upon their sleep,
And, poet in your music keep
Their memory alive and fair,
Echoing through the electric air.

5

What will you do with your shovel, Dai,
And your pick and your sledge and your spike,
And what will you do with your leisure, man,
Now that you're out on strike?

What will you do for your butter, Dai,
And your bread and your cheese and your fags,
And how will you pay for a dress for the wife,
And shall your children go in rags?

You have been, in your time, a hero, Dai,
And they wrote of your pluck in the press,
And now you have fallen on evil days,
And who will be there to bless?

And how will you stand with your honesty, Dai,
When the land is full of lies,
And how will you curb your anger, man,
When your natural patience dies?

O what will you dream on the mountains, Dai,
When you walk in the summer day,
And gaze on the derelict valleys below,
And the mountains farther away?

And how will the heart within you, Dai,
Respond to the distant sea,
And the dream that is born in the blaze of the sun,
And the vision of victory?

7

Mrs Evans fach, you want butter again.
How will you pay for it now, little woman
With your husband out on strike, and full
Of the fiery language? Ay, I know him,
His head is full of fire and brimstone
And a lot of palaver about communism,
And me, little Dan the Grocer
Depending so much on private enterprise.

What, depending on the miners and their
Money too? O yes, in a way, Mrs Evans,
Yes, in a way I do, mind you.
Come tomorrow, little woman, and I'll tell you then
What I have decided overnight.
Go home now and tell that rash red husband of
                                    yours
That your grocer cannot afford to go on strike
Or what would happen to the butter from
                                    Carmarthen?
Good day for now, Mrs Evans fach.

10

High summer on the mountains
And on the clover leas,
And on the local sidings,
And on the rhubarb leaves.

Brass bands in all the valleys
Blaring defiant tunes,
Crowds, acclaiming carnival,
Prize pigs and wooden spoons.

Dust on shabby hedgerows
Behind the colliery wall,
Dust on rail and girder
And tram and prop and all.

High summer on the slag heaps
And on polluted streams,
And old men in the morning
Telling the town their dreams.

13

O the lands of Usk are dear
    And all the woods of Wye,
And the magic shores of Dyfed
    Beneath the summer sky.

But the blackened slopes of Rhymney
    I saw with childhood's eye,
These shall be dearer, dearer,
    When I must turn to die.

15

In the square brown chapel below the hill
Dai's frail mother is deep in prayer,
A broken old mother who bears no ill
To anyone anywhere.

'Please God have blessings for us all
And comfort them who mourn,
And have mercy on me in my humble shawl,
And melt the hearts of stone.'

The sun's last light is passing away,
And a moth flits to and fro,
And out in the street the children play
And the echoes softly go.

'O Brother who came from Nazareth
To help and heal and save,
O Lord of life and Lord of death,
Help my old heart to be brave.'

18

Man alive, what a belly you've got!
You'll take all the serge in my little shop.
Stand still for a minute, now, and I'll get your
                                    waist.

Man alive, what a belly you've got!
Oh, I know it's only a striker's pay you get,
But don't misunderstand me, Hywel bach;
I depend for my bread on working men
And I am only a working man myself,
Just Shinkin Rees the little tailor,
Proud of my work and the people I serve;
And I wouldn't deny you a suit for all the gold
                              in all the world.
Just pay me a little each week, Hywel bach,
And I am your tailor as long as you live,
Shinkin Rees your friend and your tailor,
Proud to serve you, and your dear old father
                              before you.
But man alive, what a belly you've got!

20

Look at the valleys down there in the darkness,
Long bracelets of twinkling lights,
And here with the mountain breeze on your brow
Consider the folk in the numberless streets
Between the long dark ridges, north to south.
Township after township lit up in long broken
                              lines,
Silent and sparkling, sprinkling with jewels the
                              night,

And Mrs Hughes and Mrs Rees rushing from
                              shop to shop,
All fuss and bother, and Gwyneth and Blodwen
And slim young men hurrying now to the sixpenny
                              dance,
And Shoni Bach Morris away to his pint,
And Ned and his wife and his kids in a crowd
Intent on the glamour of Hollywood;
Street intersecting street, and memorial clock in
                              the circle,
The chemist's window radiant with cures for all
                              complaints,
Lovers holding hands outside the furniture stores,
Bright buses sliding in from east and west,
And here's the toothless, barefoot old sailor at
                              the corner
Yelling a song for your little brown penny.
London in little for one night in the week,
Red lights and green lights, and crowded
                              pavements,
And who cares a damn on one night at least,
One night of tinsel, one night of jazz.
And one by one the lights shall go out
In the valleys, leaving isolated lamps, silver pins,
Sticking into the inverted velvet of the midnight
                              air.
And you shall listen then to the silence
That is not silence, to the murmur
Of the uneasy centuries among the ancient hills

<pre>
                              and valleys
As here you stand with the mountain breeze on
                              your brow.
</pre>

22

Shoni bach Amos drunk again!
And your whiskers long and white,
And your nose as red as a sunset
And your old, old eyes so bright.

Shoni bach Amos drunk again!
And merry as twenty-three,
Singing of cronies and wenches
And the fun that used to be.

Shoni bach Amos drunk again!
Drunk as a lord in town,
Forgetting the life-long squalor
That kept you and your children down.

24

Cow-parsley and hawthorn blossom
And a cottage among trees,
A thrush and a skylark singing,
And a gipsy lying at ease.

Roses in gentlemen's gardens
Smile as we pass by the way,
And the swans of my lord are sleeping
Out of the heat of the day.

And here we come tramping and singing
Out of the valleys of strife,
Into the sunlit cornlands,
Begging the bread of life.

25

He won't talk any more of the distant days
Of his childhood in the coalface and the tavern
And all his cronies who had left him behind
In the ragged little hut by the river;
He who had given so much of his sweat
In the days of his youth and his vigour,
Now falling like a wrinkled apple into a ditch
To rot away in the everlasting dust of death.
Tonight he shall sleep in a grave on the slope,
And no more will he prattle of the days of his
                                        youth,
Days of the Truck System and the Tory Sabbath,
And the Chartists and the starved-out strikers.
No more will he lean on the bridge in the summer
                                        morning

And make a god of Gladstone and a devil of
                                                    Disraeli,
And go into raptures on the young Lloyd George
Who strode into London with a dazzling sword,
A bright St David from the stormy mountain.
All his long and luckless days are over,
And the broken old body in the plain deal coffin
Will be deaf to all the birds above the hill,
The larks that sing and sing in the cloudless sky
As the men move away in slow black clusters
Down on the road to the colliery town.

28

Hywel and Olwen are alone in the fern
On the hills behind the town,
Talking and kissing with lips that burn
As the sun of June goes down.

'O how can we marry, Olwen, my love,
With me on a striker's pay?
How will you manage a home, my love,
Through the troubles of the day?'

'I will face all the troubles as others do,
Hywel my darling, my love,
And share in your battle through and through,
And live and die for love!'

Hywel and Olwen lie warm in the fern
With passionate mouth on mouth
And the lights in the valley twinkle and turn
And the moon climbs up from the south.

29

In the Admiral Nelson the lads are together,
And Lizzie the barmaid is rippling with fun,
And on Saturday night the beer is good.

The darts whizz past the full flushed faces,
And the old men chuckle with yellow teeth,
And on Saturday night the beer is good.

The fiddler's mate crawls round with a cap,
'Our Tommy is going to college some day',
And on Saturday night the beer is good.

The sawdust is bright for the first half hour,
'Lloyd George was the boy to talk to the Lords',
And on Saturday night the beer is good.

The curate calls in for a box of matches,
'My old Martha was full of the devil today',
And on Saturday night the beer is good.

Let's go to Barry Island, Maggie fach,
And give all the kids one day by the sea,
And sherbert and buns and paper hats,
And a rattling ride on the Figure Eight;
We'll have tea on the sands, and rides on the
                                    donkeys,
And sit in the evening with the folk of
                        Cwm Rhondda,
Singing the sweet old hymns of Pantycelyn
When the sun goes down beyond the rocky islands.
Come on, Maggie fach, or the train will be gone
Then the kids will be howling at home all day,
Sticky with dirt and gooseberry jam.
Leave the washing alone for today, Maggie fach,
And put on your best and come out to the sun
And down to the holiday sea.
We'll carry the sandwiches in a big brown bag
And leave our troubles behind for a day
With the chickens and the big black tips
And the rival soup-kitchens, quarrelling like hell.
Come, Maggie fach, with a rose on your breast
And an old Welsh tune on your little red lips,
And we'll all sing together in the Cardiff train
Down to the holiday sea.

36

In the little Italian shop
Where they sell coloured gassy pop,
Listen to Emlyn tell his mate
How to organise the State,
How to end the troublous days
And lead the world to wiser ways.
Danny bach Dwl is eager, too,
To put an end to ballyhoo;
And Nipper Evans would put things right
In this nation overnight.
One would make things brisk and hot,
Another kill the whole damn lot . . .
And on and on the chatter flows
Until Maria yawns and goes
To pull the blinds and shut the shop
So full of coloured gassy pop.

37

Send out your homing pigeons, Dai,
Your blue-grey pigeons, hard as nails,
Send them with messages tied to their wings,
Words of your anger, words of your love.
Send them to Dover, to Glasgow, to Cork,
Send them to the wharves of Hull and of Belfast,
To the harbours of Liverpool and Dublin and Leith,

Send them to the islands and out of the oceans,
To the wild wet islands of the northern sea
Where little grey women go out in heavy shawls
At the hour of dusk to gaze on the merciless waters,
And send them to the decorated islands of the
                                                    south
Where the mineowner and his tall stiff lady
Walk round and round the rose-pink hotel, day
                                    after day after day.
Send out your pigeons, Dai, send them out
With words of your anger and your love and
                                        your pride,
With stern little sentences wrought in your heart,
Send out your pigeons, flashing and dazzling
                                    towards the sun.

Go out, pigeons bach, and do what Dai tells you.

38

From Ammanford to Fleur-de-Lys
No honest man will bend the knee
To any parasitic band
Which battens on the ravaged land.

From Dowlais Top to Swansea Bay
The men are in the sun today
With angry hearts and fists of fire
To meet the challenge of the squire.

From Blaina down to Barry Dock
Dai and Glyn have set the clock
That points unto the judgement hour
For the vandal in his tower.

41

Here is Arthur J. Cook, a red rose in his lapel,
Astride on a wall, arousing his people,
Now with fist in the air, now a slap to the knee,
Almost burning his way to victory!

And tomorrow in all the hostile papers
There will be sneers at Cook and all his capers,
And cowardly scribblers will be busy tonight
Besmirching a warrior with the mud of their spite.

O rain of July pouring down from the heavens,
Pouring and pelting from the vaults of the sky,
Pelting and slashing and lashing the trees,
Lashing the gardens behind the streets,
Sweeping the dust from the cabbage leaves,
And bringing Mrs Hughes' pet geranium out to
                              the garden wall,
Sweep away, thunder-rain, the dross from our
                              valleys,
Carry the rubbish to the seas and the oceans,
Wash away the slag-heaps of our troubles and
                              sorrows,
Sweep away, thunder-rain, the slime from our
                              valleys,
And let our streets, our home, our visions
Be cleansed and be shining when the evening
                              comes
With its rainbow arching the smiling uplands,
With its glittering trees and laughing flowers,
And its mountains bright with the setting sun.

44

You men of Gwent and Gwalia
From Neath to Ebbw Vale,
Sing us a song of triumph
Out of a Celtic tale.

Sing to the crowded valleys
Anthems of heaven and earth,
Stir the blood within us
And flood our hearts with mirth.

You tenors from Treorchy,
Basses from Abercwmboi,
Sing to the hills and valleys,
Rouse all the people to joy.

47

In Capel Hebron the choirs are singing,
And Martha and Jane and Hywel and Emrys
Are lost in the rapture of anthem and chorus
And the walls of the chapel are shaking with song,
And wave after wave of music crashes
Over the maddened multitude.
Chorus of Handel, mighty and glorious,
Rolls and reverberates again and again,
Tearing the barriers and bastions asunder,

Shaking the heart and the depths of the soul.
O spirit of music and wonder and passion
Flood with thy rapture our derelict valleys,
And give unto men the motive to action,
The impulse to build what is worthy of man.

48

The telephones are ringing
And treachery's in the air.
The sleek one,
The expert at compromise,
Is bowing in Whitehall.
And lackey to fox to parrot cries:
'The nation must be saved.'
What is the nation, gentlemen,
Who are the nation, my lords?
The sleek one,
The expert at compromise,
Is chattering in Whitehall.
The men who have made this nation,
Who have made her gross in wealth,
The men who have given their flesh and blood
From century to century,
They do not scream and panic,
They do not cringe and whine,
They do not shudder in the hour of crisis.
It is the robber and the gambler and the parasite

Who yell when the hour of reckoning comes.
But the sleek one,
The expert at compromise,
Is signing in Whitehall.
The buying and selling is over,
The treachery sealed, and called
A national triumph;
And this Friday goes down to history
Yellow, and edged with black.

Tonypandy

I

Dai bach, Dai bach, with your woollen muffler
Tight around your stout dark neck,
Why do you seem so sad and lonely
There at the corner of Pandy Square,
Now in this moist grey hour of twilight
And colourless streets and long black hills?
Are your eyes on those birds that have strayed
                                      from the sea,
Those few smooth gulls up from the Severn,
Floating and crying below the clouds,
Complaining and floating above the valley-sides?
Do the sea-birds awaken old sorrows at dusk
There at the corner of Pandy Square,
As they circle and sigh above the slag-heaps
And the narrow brown river trickling
Between the crooked streets and the colliery
                                      sidings?
Are they as poems from the Severn Sea,
Sad little lyrics borne on the dusk wind
Over the coastal plain and over the valleys
Up to the mountains and mists of Glamorgan,
Haunting the twilight, haunting the heart?
Or do they remind you, David, you son of
                                      Tonypandy,
Of summer afternoons on holiday beaches,

And cheap excursions to Weston-super-Mare,
With the steamer chuff-chuff-chuffing across the
                                        Channel
And the Flatholm in the distance, and the sunshine
Radiant over the Somerset cliffs and gardens,
And your Martha, with her mouth wide open,
Leaning against you on the crowded deck,
And the Sunday School parties all around you
Sweating with singing the sad, sad hymns?
And O it was sweet in the evening, Dai,
After the bathing and the dancing and the pastries
                                        and the ice-cream,
And the gardens of roses behind the coloured
                                        town,
And the nut-brown ale in the pub by the pier,
Ay, it was sweet upon the evening waters
To watch the sun go down in scarlet
Behind the far promontory, and gaze upon
The velvet undulations of the sea,
And sweet it was to dream,
To watch the sun go down in scarlet
Behind the far promontory, and gaze upon
The velvet undulations of the sea,
And sweet it was to dream, Dai bach,
With Martha warm and fragrant, close against you,
Martha from Treorchy nestled in your arms,
Sweet it was to coo of love and summer
To the rhythm and the moaning of the darkening
                                        sea,

And the pleasure-boat chuff-chuff-chuffing
                                        homewards
Toward the lights of Cardiff in the bluish distance,
And the waiting quays and the quayside station,
With your Day Excursion tickets sticky in your
                                        hands.
Or do I dream that you dream like this
There as you stand in the dreary dusk,
There at the corner of Pandy Square?

II

When you were young, Dai, when you were
                                        young!
The Saturday mornings of childhood
With childish dreams and adventures
Among the black tips by the river,
And the rough grass and the nettles
Behind the colliery yard, the stone-throwing
Battles between the ragged boys,
The fascination of the railway cutting
On dusty summer afternoons,
And the winter night and its street-lamps
And the first pranks of love,
And the deep warm sleep
In grandmother's chapel pew
On stodgy Sunday evenings,
And the buttercup-field you sometimes noticed

Behind the farthest street, the magical field
That only the heart could see,
The heart and rarely the boyish eye,
And the pride you had in your father's
Loins and shoulders when he bent
Between the tub and the fire,
And the days you counted, counted, counted,
Before you should work in the mine.
You never, never cursed your luck
Or desired to see another town or valley,
Or know any other men and women
Than those of the streets around
The street where you were born.
Your world was narrow and magical
And dear and dirty and brave
When you were young, Dai, when you were
                                        young!

III

The dusk deepens into the autumn night,
The cold drizzle spreads across the valleys,
The rubbish heaps are lost among the mists,
And where will you go for the evening, Dai,
For the evening in Tonypandy?
Will you count your coppers and join
The cinema queue where the tired women
Huddle like sheep, and comfort one another

With sighs and sentimental phrases,
And where some folk blame the local councillors
For all the evils of the day and night?
O in the little queue, what tales are told
When we have shuffled off the burdens of the day –
What rancour, what compassion, what relief!
Or perhaps you will go to the prayer meeting down
the chapel,
Where the newest member can pray for an hour
without stopping,
The one converted at the last Big Meeting.
Or will you go to the pub at the corner
Where tongues come loose and hearts grow soft,
Where politics are so easy to understand,
Where the Irish labourer explains the constitution
of de Valera,
And the Tory Working Man snarls behind his beer
At those who do not worship Winston Churchill,
And those who vaguely praise the Beveridge
Report.
Or perhaps you will go back to your fireside this
evening
And talk with your Martha of the children abroad,
The son out in Italy, the quick-tongued Ifor,
And the young quiet Emrys in the R.A.F.,
And Mair, with her roses and her laughing eyes,
So sprightly in her khaki uniform;
And you will be proud and you will be sad,
And you will be brave for Martha's sake,
And you will be Dai the great of heart.

IV

So much you have given, so little received,
O Dai, you miner of Tonypandy!
And 'blessed it is to give' the Bible says –
My God, then you ought to be an angel,
An angel in the Garden of Empire,
With wings of Red, White and Blue!
But to-night as you sit by your kitchen fire
You know in your heart how your life has been
                                        botched,
Been robbed of peace and grace and beauty,
Of leisure to dream and build and create,
Not the leisure of the shabby witless idler,
But the leisure that burgeons with proud
                                        achievement,
The leisure that marks an awakened nation
Exultantly singing the joy of the earth.
How silently and subtly and surely the chains
Have bound the mind and the body
To the status quo of the iron jungle!
Men have gone down unknown through the ages,
Down to the shame that is deeper than death,
Darkness behind them, darkness before them,
Ravaged by hunger to desperation
And goaded and whipped and tortured
For the sake of a pampered despotic few.
And here in your home in Tonypandy,
To-night by this fire that flickers and dies,

You know that these words are not figures of fancy,
You know that they echo the thoughts in your
                                            heart.

V

Dai in his bed and Tonypandy
Silent under the silent stars,
Silent and black and cold beneath the autumn
                                            night,
The night so full of mystery and memory,
The night of stars above the streets of Tonypandy:
And you shall listen to the footsteps crossing
                              Pandy Square,
The echoes of the footsteps silenced long ago,
Dear, dogged footsteps marching to the sound of
                              drum and fife,
Footsteps whose echoes were heard across the
                                            mountains,
Footsteps of toilers and rebels and dreamers,
And the echoes of bullets and galloping horses
And curses and desperate rallying calls.
And older far than all those echoes
You hear the battle cries of Celtic kings
And bearded chieftains in the virgin valleys
Riding in scarlet and yellow to the castles by the
                                            Severn Sea.

And the skies that look down to-night and to-
                                        morrow
On slag-heaps and hovels and little bowler-hatted
                                        deacons,
On square grey chapels and gasometers and pubs,
Once saw Cadwgan and his shining battle-axe
Rallying his warriors among the summer
                                        mountains,
And Owain Glyndŵr sweeping southward to the
                                        feudal coast,
With colour and with music and with pride
And Dai's forefathers roused by song and banner
Alive to the passionate lore of Gwalia,
Crowding and flocking and roaring to battle
Between the hills and the forests and the Severn
                                        Sea,
Martyrs to freedom and the Celtic dream.
And will that dream disturb one sleeping youth
                                        to-night
Beneath the roofs, among the streets of
                                        Tonypandy?
And shall the Future mock our simple, simple faith
In the Progress that has scorned the native culture,
The legend and the vision and the dream,
And a people that has nigh lost its history and
                                        language
To serve with blood and flesh the maw of
                                        Mammon?
O singers, singers in a thousand years to be,

Who shall sing of joys our richest hearts can never
conceive,
Forget not the dreams of the few who dream
to-night
Among the rubbish heaps of 1944!
And forgive and pity and remember those
Whose souls were narrowed by the joyless day,
The lack of bread, the sordid strife,
The penury inherited from father to son to son,
And men in chains who did not feel the chains.
And singers, singers in a distant golden time to be,
Remember a little of Dai and Tonypandy,
Dai and his Martha and his fireside,
Dai and his lamp in the depths of the earth,
Dai and his careless lilting tongue.
Dai and his heart of gold.

VI

And meanwhile, Dai, with your woollen muffler
Tight around your pit-scarred neck,
Remind us of the gratitude we owe you,
We who so easily pass you by.

Remind us of your long endurance,
Those bitter battles the sun has never seen,
And remind us of the struggles you have waged
Against the crude philosphy of greed.

And remind all who strut with noses high in the air,
How the proudest of nations would falter without
                                                    you,
And remind us when we lie on fireside cushions
Of the blood that is burnt within the flame.

And remind us when we kneel to the unknown
                                        God
And turn and cry to the cold infinite heavens,
Remind us of the toil of the blistered hands
And the courage and the comradeship of men.

The Lay Preacher Ponders

'Isn't the violet a dear little flower? And the daisy,
                                                too.
What nice little thoughts arise from a daisy!
If I were a poet now – but no, not a poet,
For a poet is a wild and blasphemous man;
He talks about wine and women too much for me
And he makes mad songs about old pagans,
                                        look you.
Poets are dangerous men to have in chapel,
And it is bad enough in chapel as it is
With all the quarrelling over the organ and the
                                        deacons;
The deacons are not too nice to saintly young men
                                        like me.
(Look at Jenkin John Jones, the old damn
                                scoundrel!)
They know I can pray for hours and hours,
They know what a righteous young man I am,
They know how my Bible is always in my pocket
And Abraham and Jonah like brothers to me,
But they prefer the proper preacher with his collar
                                        turned round;
They say he is more cultured than I am,
And what is culture but palaver and swank?
I turn up my nose at culture.
I stand up for faith, and very simple faith,
And knowledge I hate because it is poison.

Think of this devilish thing they call science,
It is Satan's new trick to poison men's minds.
When I shall be local councillor and a famous
                                        man –
I look forward to the day when I shall be mayor –
I will put my foot down on clever palaver,
And show what a righteous young man I am.
And they ought to know I am that already,
For I give all my spare cash to the chapel
And all my spare time to God.'

The Ballad of a Bounder

He addressed great congregations
And rolled his tongue with grease,
And his belly always flourished,
In time of war or peace.

He would talk of distant comrades
And brothers o'er the sea,
And snarl above his liquor
About neighbours two or three.

He knew a lot about public money –
More than he liked to say –
And sometimes sat with the paupers
To increase his Extra pay.

He could quote from Martin Tupper
And Wilhelmina Stitch,
And creep from chapel to bargain
With the likeliest local bitch.

He could swindle and squeal and snivel
And cheat and chant and pray,
And retreat like a famous general
When Truth would bar his way.

But God grew sick and tired
Of such a godly soul,
And sent down Death to gather
His body to a hole.

But before he died, the Bounder
Said: 'My children, be at peace;
I know *I* am going to heaven,
So rub my tongue with grease.'

Marx and Heine and Dowlais

I used to go to St John's Wood
On Saturday evenings in summer
To look on London behind the dusty garden trees,
And argue pleasantly and bitterly
About Marx and Heine, the iron brain and the
                                    laughing sword;
And the ghost of Keats would sit in a corner,
Smiling slowly behind a summer of wine,
Sadly smiling at the fires of the future.
And late in the summer night
I heard the tall Victorian critics snapping
Grim grey fingers at London Transport,
And sober, solemn students of James Joyce,
Dawdling and hissing into Camden Town.

But now in the winter dusk
I go to Dowlais Top
And stand by the railway bridge
Which joins the bleak brown hills,
And gaze at the streets of Dowlais
Lop-sided on the steep dark slope,
A battered bucket on a broken hill,
And see the rigid phrases of Marx
Bold and black against the steel-grey west,
Riveted along the sullen skies.
And as for Heine, I look on the rough
Bleak, colourless hills around,

Naked and hard as flint,
Romance in a rough chemise.

Rhymney
(For Ceinfryn and Gwyn)

When April came to Rhymney
With shower and sun and shower,
The green hills and the brown hills
Could sport some simple flower,
And sweet it was to fancy
That even the blackest mound
Was proud of its single daisy
Rooted in bitter ground.

And old men would remember
And young men would be vain,
And the hawthorn by the pithead
Would blossom in the rain,
And the drabbest streets of evening,
They had their magic hour,
When April came to Rhymney
With shower and sun and shower.

Tiger Bay

I watched the coloured seamen in the morning
                                                                    mist,
Slouching along the damp brown street,
Cursing and laughing in the dismal dawn.
The sea had grumbled through the night,
Small yellow lights had flickered far and near,
Huge chains clattered on the ice-cold quays,
And daylight had seemed a hundred years away . . .
But slowly the long cold night retreated
Behind the cranes and masts and funnels,
The sea-signals wailed beyond the harbour
And seabirds came suddenly out of the mist.
And six coloured seamen came slouching along
With the laughter of the Levant in their eyes
And contempt in their tapering hands.
Their coffee was waiting in some smoke-laden den,
With smooth yellow dice on the unswept table,
And behind the dirty green window
No lazy dream of Africa or Arabia or India,
Nor any dreary dockland morning
Would mar one minute for them.

London Welsh

We have scratched our names in the London dust,
Sung sometimes like the Jews of Babylon
Under the dusty trees of Hyde Park Corner,
Almost believing in a Jesus of Cardigan
Or a Moses on the mountains of Merioneth;
We have dreamed by the Thames of Towy and Dee,
And whistled in dairy shops in the morning,
Whistled of Harlech and Aberdovey.
We have grown sentimental in London
Over things that we smiled at in Wales.
Sometimes in Woolwich we have seen the mining
                                        valleys
More beautiful than we ever saw them with our
                                        eyes.
We have carried our accents into Westminster
As soldiers carry rifles into the wars;
We have carried our idioms into Piccadilly,
Food for the critics on Saturday night.
We have played dominoes in Lambeth with Alfred
                                        the Great,
And lifted a glass with Henry VIII
In the tavern under the railway bridge
On Friday nights in winter;
And we have argued with Chaucer down the Old
                                        Kent Road
On the englynion of the Eisteddfod.
We have also shivered by the Thames in the night
And known that the frost has no racial distinctions.

In Gardens in the Rhondda

In gardens in the Rhondda
    The daffodils dance and shine
When tired men trudge homeward
    From factory and mine.

The daffodils dance in gardens
    Behind the grim brown row
Built among the slagheaps
    In a hurry long ago.

They dance as though in passion
    To shame and to indict
The brutes who built so basely
    In the long Victorian night.

I was born in Rhymney

I was born in Rhymney
To a miner and his wife –
On a January morning
I was pulled into this Life.

Among Anglicans and Baptists
And Methodists I grew,
And my childhood had to chew and chance
The creed of such a crew.

I went to church and chapel
Ere I could understand
That Apollo rules the heavens
And Mammon rules the land.

And I woke on many mornings
In a little oblong room,
And saw the frown of Spurgeon:
'Beware, my boy, of doom.'

And there was the family Bible
Beneath a vase of flowers,
With pictures of the Holy Land
That enchanted me for hours.

And there was my Uncle Edward,
Solemn and stern and grey,
A Calvinistic Methodist
Who made me kneel and pray.

He would carry me on his shoulders
When I was six or seven
And tell me of the golden days
When chariots flew to heaven.

He was furious against Pharaoh
And scornful about Eve,
But his pathos about Joseph
Could always make me grieve.

He knew the tribes and custom
And the apt geography
Of Jerusalem and Jericho
And the hills of Galilee.

And Moses was his hero
And Jehovah was his God.
And his stories were as magical
As Aaron's magic rod.

But sometimes from the Bible
He would turn to politics
And tell of Gladstone's glory
And Disraeli's little tricks.

But even William Ewart Gladstone
Of beloved memory
Would fade and be forgotten
When it came to D.L.G.

The little Celt from Criccieth,
The Liberal on fire,
He was the modern Merlin
And Moses and Isaiah!

The ghost of Uncle Edward
In a solemn bowler hat,
Does it haunt the plains of Moab
Or the slopes of Ararat?

Or lurks it in the Gateway,
Where Peter holds the key,
To welcome on the harp strings
The ghost of D.L.G.?

I lost my native language
For the one the Saxon spake
By going to school by order
For education's sake.

I learnt the use of decimals,
And where to place the dot,
Four or five lines from Shakespeare
And twelve from Walter Scott.

I learnt a little grammar,
And some geography,
Was frightened of perspective,
And detested poetry.

In a land of narrow valleys,
And solemn Sabbath Days,
And collieries and choirs,
I learnt my people's ways.

I looked on local deacons
With not a little awe,
I waved a penny Union Jack
When Asquith went to war.

I pinned my faith in Kitchener
And later in Haig and Foch,
And pitied little Belgium
And cursed the bloody Boche.

We warred along the hillsides
And volleyed sticks and stones,
And sometimes smashed the windows
Of Mrs Hughes and Jones.

We stood in queues for apples,
For paraffin, and jam,
And were told to spit on Lenin,
And honour Uncle Sam.

But often in the evenings
When all the stars were out
We played beneath the lamp-post
And did not stop to doubt

That the world was made for children
Early on Christmas Day
By a jolly old whiskered Josser
In a mansion far away.

And there were the hours for Chaplin,
Pearl White, and Buffalo Bill,
And the hours for nests and whinberries
High on the summer hill.

And O the hour of lilac
And a leopard in the sky,
And the heart of childhood singing
A song that cannot die!

I learnt of Saul and Jesus
In the little Sunday School,
And later learnt to muse and doubt
By some lonely mountain pool.

I saw that creeds could comfort
And hypocrisy console
But in my blood were battles
No Bible could control.

And I praised the unknown Artist
Of crag and fern and stream
For the sunshine on the mountains
And the wonder of a dream.

On one February morning,
Unwillingly I went
To crawl in moleskin trousers
Beneath the rocks of Gwent.

And a chubby little collier
Grew fat on sweat and dust,
And listened to heated arguments
On God and Marx and lust.

For seven years among the colliers
I learnt to laugh and curse,
When times were fairly prosperous
And when they were ten times worse.

And I loved and loved the mountains
Against the cloudy sky,
The sidings, and the slag-heaps
That sometimes hurt the eye.

MacDonald was my hero,
The man who seemed inspired,
The leader with a vision,
Whose soul could not be hired!

I quoted from his speeches
In the coalface to my friends –
But I lived to see him selling
Great dreams for little ends.

And there were strikes and lock-outs
And meetings in the Square,
When Cook and Smith and Bevan
Electrified the air.

But the greatest of our battles
We lost in '26
Through treachery and lying,
And Baldwin's box of tricks.

I began to read from Shelley
In afternoons in May,
And to muse upon the misery
Of unemployment pay.

I stood in queues for hours
Outside the drab Exchange,
With my hands deep in my pockets
In a suit I could not change.

I stood before Tribunals
And smothered all my pride,
And bowed to my inferiors,
And raged with my soul outside.

And I walked my native hillsides
In sunshine and in rain,
And learnt the poet's language
To ease me of my pain.

With Wordsworth and with Shelley
I scribbled out my dreams,
Sometimes among the slag-heaps,
Sometimes by mountain streams.

O I shook hands with Shelley
Among the moonlit fern,
And he smiled, and slowly pointed
To the heart that would not burn.

And I discovered Milton
In a shabby little room
Where I spent six summer evenings
In most luxurious gloom.

I met Macbeth and Lear,
And Falstaff full of wine,
And I went one day to Stratford
To tread on ground divine.

And I toiled through dismal evenings
With algebraical signs,
With Euclid and Pythagoras
And all their points and lines.

Sometimes there came triumph
But sometimes came despair,
And I would fling all books aside
And drink the midnight air.

And there were dark and bitter mornings
When the streets like coffins lay
Between the winter mountains,
Long and bleak and grey.

But season followed season
And beauty never died
And there were days and hours
Of hope and faith and pride.

In springtime I went roaming
Along the Severn Sea,
Rejoicing in the tempest
And its savage ecstasy.

And there were summer evenings
By Taf, and Usk, and Wye,
When the land was bright with colour
Beneath a quiet sky.

But always home to Rhymney
From wandering I came,
Back to the long and lonely
Self-tuition game,

Back to Euclid's problems,
And algebraical signs,
And the route of trade and commerce,
And Caesar's battle lines,

Back to the lonely evenings
Of triumph and despair
In a little room in Rhymney
With a hint of mountain air.

O days I shall remember
Until I drop and die! –
Youth's bitter sweet progression
Beneath a Rhymney sky.

At last I went to college,
To the city on the Trent,
In the land of D.H. Lawrence
And his savage Testament.

And history and poetry
Filled all my days and nights,
And in the streets of Nottingham
I harnessed my delights.

I loved the leafy villages
Along the winding Trent,
And sometimes sighed at sunset
For the darker hills of Gwent.

And the churches of East Anglia
Delighted heart and eye,
The little steepled churches
Against the boundless sky.

And lecture followed lecture
In the college by the lake,
And some were sweet to swallow
And some were hard to take.

I read from Keats and Lawrence,
And Eliot, Shaw, and Yeats,
And the 'History of Europe
With diagrams and dates'.

I went to Sherwood Forest
To look for Robin Hood,
But little tawdry villas
Were where the oaks once stood.

And I heard the ghost of Lawrence
Raging in the night
Against the thumbs of Progress
That botched the land with blight.

And season followed season
And beauty never died,
And I left the land of Trent again
To roam by Rhymney's side,

By the narrow Rhymney River
That erratically flows
Among the furnace ruins
Where the sullen thistle blows.

Then I tried for posts in Yorkshire,
In Staffordshire and Kent,
For hopeless was the striving
For any post in Gwent.

I wrote out testimonials
Till my hands began to cry
That the world was full of jackals
And beasts of smaller fry.

At last, at last, in London
On one November day,
I began to earn my living,
To weave my words for pay.

At last I walked in London,
In park and square and street,
In bright and shady London
Where all the nations meet.

At last I lived in London
And saw the sun go down
Behind the mists of Richmond
And the smoke of Camden Town.

I watched the King of England
Go riding with his queen,
I watched the cats steal sausage
From stalls in Bethnal Green.

I tried the air of Hampstead,
I tried the brew of Bow,
I tried the cake of Kensington
And the supper of Soho.

I rode in trams and taxis
And tried the social round
And hurried home to Highgate
On the London Underground.

In little rooms in London
The poetry of Yeats
Was my fire and my fountain –
And the fury of my mates.

I found cherries in Jane Austen
And grapes in Hemingway,
And truth more strange than fiction
In the streets of Holloway.

And da Vinci and El Greco
And Turner and Cézanne,
They proved to me the splendour
And divinity of man.

I gazed at stones from Hellas,
And heard imagined trees
Echo across the ages
The words of Sophocles.

And often of a Sunday
I hailed the highest art,
The cataracts and gardens
Of Wagner and Mozart.

I studied Marx and Engels,
And put Berkeley's theme aside,
And listened to the orators
Who yelled and cooed and cried.

O the orators, the orators,
On boxes in the parks,
They judge the Day of Judgment
And award Jehovah marks.

O the orators, the orators,
When shall their voices die?
When London is a soap-box
With its bottom to the sky.

In many a public library
I watched the strong men sleep,
And virgins reading volumes
Which made their blushes deep.

Sometimes I watched the Commons
From the narrow galleries,
My left eye on the Premier,
My right on the Welsh MPs.

In Christopher Wren's Cathedral
I heard Dean Inge lament
The lack of care in breeding
From Caithness down to Kent.

And once in the ancient Abbey
I heard Thomas Hardy sigh:
'O why must a Wessex pagan
Here uneasily lie?'

To Castle Street Baptist Chapel
Like the prodigal son I went
To hear the hymns of childhood
And dream of a boy in Gwent,

To dream of far-off Sundays
When for me the sun would shine
On the broken hills of Rhymney
And the palms of Palestine.

With Tory and with Communist,
With atheist and priest,
I talked and laughed and quarrelled
Till light lit up the east.

The colonel and his nonsense,
The busman and his cheek,
I liked them all in London
For seven days a week.

O sometimes I was merry
In Bloomsbury and Kew,
When fools denied their folly
And swore that pink was blue.

And sometimes I lounged sadly
By the River in the night
And watched a body diving
And passing out of sight.

When the stars were over London
And lights lit up the Town,
I banished melancholy
And kept the critic down.

When the moon was bright on Eros
And the cars went round and round,
The whore arrived from Babylon
By the London Underground.

O I stood in Piccadilly
And sat in Leicester Square,
And mused on satin and sewerage
And lice and laissez-faire.

I saw some royal weddings
And a Silver Jubilee,
And a coloured Coronation,
And a King who crossed the sea.

In springtime to the shires
I went happy and alone,
And entered great cathedrals
To worship glass and stone.

I had holidays in Eire
Where the angels drink and dance,
And with a Tam from Ayrshire
I roamed the South of France.

For week-ends in the winter
When cash was pretty free,
I went to stay in Hastings
To argue by the sea.

For Sussex in the winter
Was dearer to me
Than Sussex full of trippers
Beside the summer sea.

In the wreck of Epping Forest
I listened as I lay
To the language of the Ghetto
Behind a hedge of May

And in the outer suburbs
I heard in the evening rain
The cry of Freud the prophet
On love and guilt and pain.

And on the roads arterial,
When London died away,
The poets of the Thirties
Were singing of decay.

I saw the placards screaming
About Hitler and his crimes,
Especially on Saturdays –
That happened many times.

And I saw folk digging trenches
In 1938,
In the dismal autumn drizzle
When all things seemed too late.

And Chamberlain went to Munich,
An umbrella at his side,
And London lost her laughter
And almost lost her pride.

I saw the crowds parading
And heard the angry cries
Around the dusty monuments
That gazed with frozen eyes.

The lands were full of fear,
And Hitler full of scorn,
And London full of critics
Whose nerves were badly torn.

And crisis followed crisis
Until at last the line
Of battle roared to fire
In 1939.

And then evacuation,
And London under fire,
And London in the distance,
The city of desire.

And the world is black with battle
In 1943,
And the hymn of hate triumphant
And loud from sea to sea.

And in this time of tumult
I can only hope and cry
That season shall follow season
And beauty shall not die.

Capel Calvin

There's holy holy people
They are in capel bach –
They don't like surpliced choirs,
They don't like Sospan Fach.

They don't like Sunday concerts,
Or women playing ball,
They don't like Williams Parry much
Or Shakespeare at all.

They don't like beer or bishops,
Or pictures without texts,
They don't like any other
Of the nonconformist sects.

And when they go to Heaven
They won't like that too well,
For the music will be sweeter
Than the music played in Hell.

A Star in the East

When Christmastide to Rhymney came
    And I was six or seven
I thought the stars in the eastern sky
    Were the brightest stars of heaven.

I chose the star that glittered most
    To the east of Rhymney town
To be the star above the byre
    Where Mary's babe lay down.

And nineteen hundred years would meet
    Beneath a magic light,
And Rhymney share with Bethlehem
    A star on Christmas night.

Hywel and Blodwen

Where are you going to, Hywel and Blodwen,
With your eyes as sad as your shoes?
We are going to learn a nimble language
By the waters of the Ouse.

We are tramping through Gloucester and through
Leicester,
We hope we shall not drop,
And we talk as we go of the Merthyr streets
And a house at Dowlais Top.

We have triads and englyns from pagan Dyfed
To brace us in the fight,
And three or four hundred Methodist hymns
To sing on a starless night.

We shall grumble and laugh and trudge together
Till we reach the stark North Sea
And talk till we die of Pantycelyn
And the eighteenth century.

We shall try to forget the Sunday squabbles,
And the foreign magistrate,
And the stupid head of the preacher's wife,
And the broken iron gate.

So here we say farewell and wish you
Less trouble and less pain,
And we trust you to breed a happier people
Ere our blood flows back again.

Come to our Revival Meeting

And this is the sordid dream of the drunkard
                              creeping to prayer,
And the maddened mob drowning the noise
                              of the birds
Frightened and fluttering in the dusty trees,
And all the hysterical converts insulting the
                              heavens,
The brown pond sticky with the thighs of the
                              damned;
And here comes a fellow to shake your liver
For out of his nightmare he leapt
When the moon crept up behind the Iron Bridge
And the garbage heap, where the trollop sat
                              waiting
To sell her filth to the fool. And I saw
All this shabby mockery of April
As a neurotic's delirium, his hallucination
Of apes and angels and dog-headed ghosts
Mingling and whirling and circling and dancing
Among the decaying boughs that laced like
                              serpents

The ripped edges of the darkening sky.

O Lord God, save us from tinned donkey,
From Soviet scientific magazines,
From the Scottish Sabbath, from American war
                                        films,
From the demagogues of Aberdare and Abadan,
And above all, O Lord God, save us from the
                                        Pentecostals.

A Carol for the Coalfield

From the moors of Blaen Rhymni down to the
                                leaning wall
Of Caerphilly Castle you shall hear the same
                                        accents
Of sorrow and mirth and pride, and a vague belief
That the future shall be greater than the past.

The man in the Rhondda Valley and the man in
                                Abertillery
Have shared the same years, the same days of hope
                                and desolation,
And in Ogmore Vale and in Ammanford both old
                                and young dream
That the future shall be greater than the past.

On the ragged hills and by the shallow polluted

                                              rivers,
The pious young man and the old rascal of many
                                              sins,
The idealists and the wasters, all sometimes believe
                                              and say
That the future shall be greater than the past.
Mothers praying for sons away in the wars, and
                                    mothers waiting
On doorsteps and by firesides for men coming
                              home from the pits,
And the old folk bent and scarred with years of toil,
                                    all sometimes hope
That the future shall be greater than the past.

Last night the moon was full above the slag heaps
                              and the grave-yards
And the towns among the hills, and a man arose
                                    from his dream
And cried out: Let this day be sufficient, and
                              worthy of my people
And let the night winds go on wailing of the future
                                    and the past.

Land of my Mothers

Land of my mothers, how shall my brothers praise
                                        you?
With timbrels or rattles or tins?
With fire.
How shall we praise you on the banks of the
                            rhymneying waters,
On the smoky shores and the glittering shores of
                                        Glamorgan,
On wet mornings in the bare fields behind the
                                Newport docks,
On fine evenings when lovers walk by Bedwellty
                                        Church,
When the cuckoo calles to miners coming home to
                                Rhymney Bridge,
When the wild rose defies the Industrial
                                Revolution
And when the dear old drunken lady sings of Jesus
                            and a little shilling.

Come down, O girls of song, to the bank of the
                                    coal canal
At twilight, at twilight
When mongrels fight
And long rats bite
Under the shadows of pit-head light,
And dance, you daughters of Gwenllian,
Dance in the dust in the lust of delight.

And you who have prayed in golden pastures
And oiled the wheels of the Western Tradition
And trod where bards have danced to church,
Pay a penny for this fragment of a burning torch.
It will never go out.

It will gather unto itself all the fires
That blaze between the heavens above and the
                                        earth beneath
Until the flame shall frighten each mud-hearted
                                        hypocrite
And scatter the beetles fattened on the cream of
                                        corruption,
The beetles that riddle the ramparts of Man.

Pay a penny for my singing torch,
O my sisters, my brothers of the land of my
                                        mothers,
The land of our fathers, our troubles, our dreams,
The land of Llewellyn and Shoni bach Shinkin,
The land of the sermons that pebble the streams,
The land of the englyn and Crawshay's old engine,
The land that is sometimes as proud as she seems.
And sons of the mountains and sons of the valleys
O lift up your hearts, and then
Lift up your feet.

For further reading

Gwalia Deserta (Dent, 1938)
The Angry Summer (Faber and Faber, 1943)
Tonypandy and other poems (Faber and Faber, 1945)
Selected Poems (Faber and Faber, 1953)
Collected Poems, ed. Islwyn Jenkins (Gomerian Press, 1972)
The Complete Poems of Idris Davies, ed. Dafydd Johnston (University of Wales Press, 1994)

Islwyn Jenkins, *Idris Davies* in the *Writers of Wales* series (University of Wales Press, 1972)
A special number of *Poetry Wales* devoted to Idris Davies (vol.16, no.4, 1981)
Islwyn Jenkins, *Idris Davies of Rhymney: a personal memoir* (Gomer, 1986)
The Angry Summer, with introduction and notes by Anthony Conran (University of Wales Press, 1993)
Fe'm ganed i yn Rhymni/I was born in Rhymney, the Idris Davies memorial volume (Gomer, 1990)

A full list of articles and reviews about the work of Idris Davies, and a selection of his own uncollected writings, will be found in John Harris, *A Bibliographical Guide to Twenty-Four Modern Anglo-Welsh Writers* (University of Wales Press, 1994).

Images of Wales

The Corgi Series covers, no. 2
'Trio against the light' by Valerie Ganz

Valerie Ganz was born in Swansea. She attended Swansea College of Art and studied painting, sculpture and stained galss. She remained as a tutor until 1973 when she turned her attention to painting full time. As her interest in the landscape of South Wales grew, her attention was drawn to the landscape of industrial areas and, in particular, the mining industry. In 1985 she took a house and studio at Six Bells, Abertillery. For nearly a year she worked at the Six Bells Colliery, alongside the miners both above ground and at the coalface. In the evening she made studies of the miners and their families at choir practice, in the snooker halls and in the chapel. The work formed the basis of many exhibitions, in particular the mining exhibition at the Glynn Vivian Gallery, Swansea in 1986, *Mining in Art* with Josef Herman, Jack Crabtree and Nicholas Evans.

A year in London followed, where she set up her studio and worked everyday at the Central School of Ballet. This was to develop still further a long held interest in figurative drawing, with a subject that had interested her for many years. Since then frequent visits to the theatre, when ballet or pantomime is being presented continues this work. She is at present working with the Ballet Russe based at the Grand Theatre, Swansea.

The Moscow State Circus on a visit to Wales was persuaded to allow her to work behind the scenes while performers rehearsed or waited to enter the ring. She found the age old excitement of the big top a fascinating subject, the clowns particularly feature in her recent work and she has since followed them to many more venues around the Country.

Recently she has become interested in Rugby as a subject for painting and has included drawings and paintings of the subject in her recent exhibitions.

Miners are still a part of her life and visits to Tower Colliery, the only deep mine in South Wales, form the basis for work on this subject.

The opening of a new drugs rehabilitation wing at Swansea Prison gave her the opportunity to have a small view of the prison and talk to some of the prisoners. This was enough to convince her that it was exactly what she wanted to study.

The governor, Vicky O'Dea was encouraging when approached, and a series of visits to every part of the prison was arranged. Over the last six months she has had total co-operation from both staff and prisoners. This has enabled her to complete the paintings and drawings presented in her latest exhibition at the Attic Gallery in Swansea, which will open on the 19th October 2002 for three weeks.

Contact details:
For enquiries, purchases or commissions, please contact Valerie Ganz:

By email at valerie@valerieganz.com
Website: www.valerieganz.com